ACKNOWLEDGEMENTS

First I would like to thank my husband, Samuel Cubbage II. Hubby, you are the one who was the guinea pig of these recipes! We had SOOO... many different dishes over the course of the Covid 19 pandemic! Thank you for always being my 'taste tester"; and helping me find just the right spices!

Thank you to MY family; The Normans. Robert and Dorothy (Dad and Mom), and Terri (my sister). After Sam, you were also guinea pigs... HAHA! Thank you for giving me such praise about my meals!

My in-laws and friends. By the time I got to try the recipes out on you, I had perfected them a bit. LOL! Thank YOU for eating my food; and making me think that it was good enough.

DEDICATION

This book is dedicated to YOU! Show your love to your family and friends, by enjoying these recipes together. A high expression of love is to share your cooking with those you hold dear. That's what I did. And I hope that this cookbook will serve you well for years to come.

Table of Contents

Chicken Dishes

1. Bobbie's Italian Ground Chicken, Rice and Eggs
2. Chicken Pot Roast
3. Chicken Piccata
4. Easy (leftover) Turkey and Chicken Pot Pie
5. Coconut Curry Chicken

Seafood Dishes

6. Bobbie's Special Crab Cakes
7. Baked Triple-Cheesy Shrimp Alfredo Pasta
8. Steel City Shrimp
9. Garlic Shrimp and Kale

Veggie Dishes

10. Veggie Pasta with Red Peppers and Kale

Pizza Dishes

11. Skillet Pizza

12. Veggie Pizza

Sausage and Ground Meat Dishes
13. Italian Sausage, Potato Skillet
14. Pulpeta

Sweet Treats

15. Pecan Banana Bread Muffins
16. Bobbie's Yummy Chocolate Brownies

Chicken Dishes

I know that this is going to sound strange. But, this is going to be a GOOD meal! You have EVERYTHING you need in it; all of the food groups. Along with BURSTING flavors... you are going to want to keep this one in your arsenal.

Bobbie's Italian Ground Chicken, Rice and Eggs

Ingredients:

- 1 lb ground chicken
- 1 teaspoon of dried basil
- 1 tablespoon of italian seasonings

Sauce

- 2 cups chicken stock (or beef stock, or veggie stock)
- ½ cup of tomato sauce
- 1 garlic clove (minced)
- 2 tablespoons of flour
- 1 tablespoon canola oil
- ½ red onion , minced
- 1 teaspoon ginger , minced
- 1 teaspoon yellow curry
- 1 cup fresh kale
- 5 large eggs

Serving:

- 2 cups steamed brown rice
- OR, you can use vegetable pasta

Instructions:

1. Mix the sauce ingredients together in a small bowl- (minus 4 of the eggs).
2. Heat the oil in a large nonstick pan until hot. Add the ground chicken. Let it cook without touching until the bottom is browned. Break up the chicken into smaller bites.
3. Add the onions and ginger. Cook, saute and stir, until the onion turns tender and the edges are lightly browned.
4. Pour in the sauce and mix. Cover and turn down the heat, and simmer for 8 minutes. Your pan should still have some sauce; enough to cover the chicken. If not, slowly stir in more broth.
5. Once the chicken is cooked, add the fresh kale greens.
6. Crack 4 eggs onto the chicken. Cover immediately. Steam the egg whites until they are cooked; and the yolks are still runny. (2 minutes).
7. Do not allow the sauce to come to a full boil, which will reduce the flour's ability to thicken the sauce. Move the pan off the heat for a few seconds if the pan gets too hot.
8. Once finished, uncover the pan and remove it from the stove. Use a spatula or ladle to transfer the ground chicken with an egg and some sauce onto a bowl of rice or pasta. Serve hot. Enjoy!

Tasty, wholesome and quite comforting. This is SOOO good!

Chicken Pot Roast

Ingredients:

- 1. 5 lb small potatoes (6 to 8), unpeeled, cut into 1-inch pieces (3 cups)
- 2 cups cut carrots
- 2 Sprigs of fresh sweet basil
- 1.5 cups chopped yellow onions
- 5 boneless skinless chicken thighs (1 1/2 lb)
- jar (12 oz) chicken gravy
- Bag of frozen green, sweet peas, thawed

Directions:

- In a slow cooker, place potatoes, carrots, basil and onions. Sprinkle chicken with seasoning salt; place over vegetables in the cooker. Pour gravy over top.
- Cover; cook on Low heat for 9 hours.
- Stir in thawed peas. Increase heat setting to High. Cover; cook about 15 minutes longer or until peas are tender. Enjoy!

Chicken Piccata

One YUMMY recipe! It's easy to make, easy to gather ingredients, and very filling! A friend was talking about making it; so, I decided to make it! And, I'm VERY happy with the results! And you will be, too!

Chicken Piccata

Ingredients:

2 skinless and boneless chicken breasts, butterflied and then cut in half
6 tablespoons unsalted butter
5 tablespoons extra-virgin olive oil
1/3 cup fresh lemon juice
1/2 cup chicken stock
1/4 cup brined capers, rinsed
1/3 cup fresh parsley, chopped
⅓ cup Fresh Basil, chopped
Seasoning salt
1 pint container of Heavy Whipping Cream
Sea salt and freshly ground black pepper to taste
1 cup of All-purpose flour

Directions:

In a large bowl, mix all- purpose flour with seasoning salt and pepper. Shake the chicken in flour and shake off excess.

1. In a large skillet over medium high heat, melt 2 tablespoons of butter with 3 tablespoons of olive oil. When butter and oil start to sizzle, add 2 pieces of chicken and cook for 4 minutes. When chicken is browned, flip and cook on the other side for 4 minutes. Remove from heat and transfer to a plate. Melt 2 more tablespoons of butter and add another 2 tablespoons of olive oil. When butter and oil start to sizzle, add the other 2 pieces of chicken and brown both sides the same way. Remove pan from heat and add chicken to the plate.

2. Into the pan add the lemon juice, stock and capers. Place back on the stove and bring to boil, scraping up brown bits from the pan for extra flavor. Check for seasoning. Return all the chicken to the pan and simmer for 5 minutes. Remove

chicken to a platter. Add remaining 2 tablespoons butter to sauce and whisk vigorously. Pour sauce over chicken and garnish with parsley.

This is what happens with leftovers here! We create other dishes! A great recipe to use some of your Thanksgiving leftovers! (Or just a Sunday dinner)!

Easy (leftover) Turkey/chicken pot pie

Ingredients:

Pre- Made Pack of Pie Crust- (Two pack)
½ Cup of Chopped Onions
½ jar of Gravy
1 Pint of Heavy Whipping Cream
2 ½ Cups of Leftover Turkey and/or Chicken
Leftover green bean casserole
Carrots
Pat of butter

Directions:

Press one of the pre-made pie crust into a pie pan. Preheat your oven at 375. Place the pie crust into the oven. Bake pie crust for 8 minutes.

While the pie crust is baking, in a large bowl, add all above ingredients, (minus the pat of butter). Lightly mix. When the pie crust is ready, add the contents of the bowl to the pie crust. Add the 2nd pie crust to the top, and with a fork, make a few poke markers. Add the pat of butter to the top of the pie.

Bake for 30 minutes. Allow to cool for 20 minutes. Serve warm. Enjoy!

A tasty dinner when you feel like you want to go on 'vacation'!

Coconut Curry Chicken

10 Chicken Tenderloins
2 tablespoons Yellow curry
½ tbs Pepper
½ tbs Seasoning Salt
½ Sugar
1 can Coconut Milk
1 Bunch Kale (Chopped)
½ Yellow Onion (Chopped)
Sour Cream
3 Pats of Butter
3 tbs Canola Oil

1 cup Basmati rice

Directions:

In a small pot, combine rice, ¾ cup water, and a pinch of salt. Bring to a boil, then cover and reduce to a low simmer. Cook until rice is tender, 15-18 minutes. Keep covered off heat until ready to serve. Use 1½ cups of water.

While the rice is cooking, wash and dry kale and onion. Remove and discard any large stems from kale. Heat the canola oil in a large skillet over medium-high heat. Add kale and onion. Saute, stirring occasionally, until tender, 5-7 minutes. Turn off the heat and transfer to a plate.

While kale cooks, season your chicken with seasoning salt. Then, cut chicken into cube sized pieces. Once kale is done, heat a little canola oil in the same pan over medium-high heat. Add chicken; saute until browned and cooked through, 6 minutes. Reduce heat to medium. Add curry. Cook, stirring, until chicken is coated, 1 minute.

Stir in coconut milk, ¼ cup water, sugar, 1 TBSP butter, and a pinch of salt. Bring to a simmer, then reduce heat to low. Cook until thickened, 2 minutes more. Add kale and sour cream; stir to combine. Taste and season with pepper. Turn off heat.

Fluff rice with a fork and season with sugar and pepper; Top rice with coconut curry chicken. Serve and Enjoy!

Seafood Dishes

Bobbie's Special Crab cakes

- 1 package of imitation crab meat
- 1 egg
- 1 cup panko bread crumbs
- ⅓ cup Mayonnaise
- Old bay seasoning
- 1 teaspoon lime juice
- ⅓ cup Red/purple onion (minced)
- 2 tbsp Minced garlic

Instructions:

1. Place crab, egg, bread crumbs, mayonnaise, Old Bay seasoning, lime juice, onions and garlic in a medium bowl and mix together thoroughly.
2. Form your mixture into 6 patties.
3. Heat 1 'pat' butter (or olive oil) over medium heat, then cook the patties until they're golden brown. It should take about 5 minutes per side.
4. You can serve these crab cakes right from the stove, or on buns and serve as sandwiches! Enjoy!

Baked Triple Cheesy Shrimp Alfredo Pasta

Ingredients:

1 cup of Kale
1 box of pasta (any kind will do)!
½ cup of Mozzarella
½ cup of Provolone
½ cup of Parmesan
1 clove of Garlic
1 dash of fresh black pepper
½ cup of Red Onions
2 bags of EXTRA Large Shrimp (Raw or Cooked is fine).

Alfredo Sauce (Store bought or you can use the recipe below for Bobbie's Homemade Alfredo Sauce)!

Directions for the meal:

Devein the shrimp and set aside. Chop one cup of kale, and set aside. Chop the garlic. In a large skillet, add 1 pat of butter to the skillet and saute the onions. When the onions are finished (about 3 minutes), add the garlic to the skillet and saute for 2 minutes. Add the kale to the skillet. Turn the heat down to low, and allow the kale to simmer with the onions and garlic. In 3 minutes, add the shrimp. Mix for about one minute. Add fresh, black pepper. Slowly add each of the cheeses, mixing the whole time. Mix for about five minutes, or until the cheese is smooth.
Add Alfredo sauce.

Bobbie's Homemade Alfredo Sauce

Ingredients:

1 pint carton of Heavy Whipping Cream
2 cloves of garlic
1 Pat of butter

1 cup of Fresh Parmesan Cheese
Directions for Sauce

In a large skillet on low heat, add the pat of butter. Chop 2 cloves of garlic, and saute the garlic in the butter.
Pour the contents of the carton of heavy whipping cream into the skillet.
As the cream starts to slowly boil, add the fresh parmesan cheese, slowly to the skillet. Mix until smooth. Turn off the heat, and set aside.

This is a recipe that I spent months trying to perfect during the pandemic. And now…. YUM!

Steel City Shrimp

Ingredients:

3 bags of extra large shrimp
1 red pepper
1 yellow pepper
1 small yellow onion
1 teaspoon of Singapore seasoning (this seasoning comes from a specialty store here in Pittsburgh. However, you can use yellow curry powder--It would be very tasty, too!)
1 cup of egg noodles
½ cup of tomato sauce
Dash of accent salt
4 tablespoons of Canola oil (for sauteing)

Directions:

In a large pot, boil the egg noodles according to the packaging. Drain the noodles when cooked, and set aside.

Finely chop the red, yellow peppers, onions. In a large pan, add the vegetables and saute the vegetables for about 5 minutes.

Clean and devein the shrimp, and cut the tails off. When you are finished, add the shrimp to the pan with the sauteed vegetables. Cook the shrimp in the sauteed vegetables for another 2 or 3 minutes. (Enough for the shrimp to turn pink.) Add the tomato sauce to the saute and mix on low heat for about 2 minutes. Add the Singapore seasoning to the mixture.

Place your cooked noodles on a plate and spoon the shrimp saute onto the noodles. Sprinkle the accent salt on top. Serve warm.

Garlic Shrimp and Kale

Ingredients:

2 Cloves of Fresh Garlic (Minced)
3 Bags of Extra Large Shrimp
2 Bunches of Kale (Chopped)
2 large Tomatoes (Chopped)
Olive oil
½ Yellow Onion (Minced)
½ tbs Seasoning Salt
Pepper (to taste)
1 Red Pepper (Chopped)
Fresh Basil (to taste)
Fresh Parsley (to taste)
½ tbs Italian Seasoning
3 Pats of Butter

Directions:

In a medium skillet, add 1 pat of butter. When the butter is melted, add the kale. Saute the kale for about 5 minutes. Add the chopped tomatoes to the skillet. Add a lid and allow the kale and tomatoes to cook for about five minutes. In a large skillet, add 2 pats of butter. When the butter is melted, saute the garlic, red pepper and onion. Add the contents from that medium skillet to the larger skillet. Add 2 teaspoons of water, add the lip and let simmer while deveining the shrimp.

When the shrimp is clean, add the olive oil to the medium skillet, and saute the shrimp for 4 minutes total. Add the shrimp to the larger skillet, add the basil, Italian seasoning, and pepper. Mix lightly. Serve warm. Enjoy!

Veggie Dishes

Veggie Pasta with Red Peppers and Kale

Ingredients:

½ Red Pepper (chopped)
1 cup of Kale (chopped)
½ cup Red Onions (chopped)
1 clove Fresh Garlic (minced)
Veggie Pasta
2 'pats' of Butter
1 pint container of Grape Tomatoes (cut each in half- horizontally)
1 sprig of Fresh Basil (chopped)
Dash of fresh Black Pepper
Salt to taste

Directions:

In a large pot, boil 3 cups of water. Once the water is bright to a boil (about 7 minutes), add veggie pasta. In a large skillet, add 2 pats of butter. When the butter has melted, add red onions, garlic and red peppers. Saute for 3 minutes, until soft. Turn the heat down to low. Add kale and tomatoes. Let simmer for about 5 minutes. Mix while simmering. Add fresh basil. At this point, the pasta should be finished. Drain the water off of the pasta. Add the pasta to the skillet. Mix for about 2 minutes- until the vegetables and pasta are mixed well. Add a dash of salt and pepper to taste. Enjoy!

PIZZA DISHES

Skillet Pizza

INGREDIENTS

- 1 pound pizza dough, at room temperature 1 hour
- 1 to 2 teaspoons vegetable or olive oil
- 1/2 to 1 cup pizza sauce
- 1 to 2 cups shredded cheese, such as mozzarella

INSTRUCTIONS

1. **Prepare the toppings.**
2. **Roll out the pizza dough.**
3. **Heat the skillet.**
4. **Cook the pizza dough for 1 minute.** Transfer the round of pizza dough to the pan. Cook until you see large bubbles forming on top and the underside shows golden spots, about 1 minute. You can deflate the bubbles with the edge of your spatula — or leave them! They'll turn into crispy bits once you flip the pizza.
5. **Flip the crust and add toppings.**
6. **Cover and reduce the heat to medium.** Cover the skillet and reduce the heat to medium. This helps the cheese melt and prevents the bottom of the pizza from burning.
7. **Cook the pizza for another 4 to 5 minutes.**

8. **Transfer to a cutting board and enjoy!**

Veggie Pizza

Ingredients:

(If you do not have time to make a pizza crust and sauce, this recipe works well with a store bought pizza shell and sauce.) However, if you would like to make your own crust and sauce, check the recipe for both below.

½ Cup or black olives
2 cloves of fresh garlic (minced)
⅓ Cup of yellow onions (chopped)
½ Cup of Mushrooms   (sliced)
⅓ Cup of Red Peppers (chopped)
⅓ Cup of Green Peppers (chopped)
½ Cup of spinach (chopped)
½ Cup of Cherry Tomatoes (sliced)

(½ Cup of mozzarella and provolone cheese mix- if you desire.)

Fresh Basil for garnish.

Directions:

Preheat your oven at 400 degrees. Add pizza dough to a lightly greased pizza pan. Bake at 400 degrees for 10 minutes, take the pizza shell out of the oven. Flip the shell over and cook on the other side for 7 minutes.

Take the shell out of the oven and add the pizza sauce (cheese) and toppings. Place back into the oven for 8 minutes. Bake until the toppings are bubbling!

Take out of the oven and let rest for 5 minutes. Serve warm.

Homemade Pizza Dough Recipe

Ingredients:
2 TBS olive oil
1 clove minced garlic
1 can of crushed tomatoes
1 teaspoon of sugar
1 teaspoon of salt
1 TBS of basil
1 TBS of oregano

Directions:

In a large pot, add all of the above ingredients. Add the pot top. Cook on low heat for 25 minutes. Mixing often. Turn off heat and let stand until ready to use.

Homemade Pizza Dough Recipe

Ingredients:

1 Package of dry yeast
1 TBS of sugar
1 Cup of warm water
2 Cups of flour (Any kind will work well with this recipe!)
1 TBS olive oil
½ teaspoon of salt

Directions:

Preheat the oven to 425. While waiting for the oven to warm up, in a medium bowl, dissolve yeast and sugar in warm water. Let stand until creamy, about 10 minutes. Stir in flour, salt and oil. Beat until smooth. Let rest for 10 minutes. Put dough out onto a lightly floured surface and roll into a round ball. Transfer crust to a lightly greased pizza pan. Bake the crust for 10 minutes, or until golden brown.

Sausage and Ground Meat Dishes

Italian Sausage Potato Skillet

INGREDIENTS:

- 1 Tbsp extra virgin olive oil
- 1 lb basil chicken sausage (any sausage can be used)
- ½ sweet onion, chopped into ½-inch pieces
- 1 lb red potatoes, chopped into ½-inch pieces
- 2 garlic cloves, minced
- 1 pint cherry tomatoes, sliced in half (divided)
- 1 Tbsp chopped rosemary
- 1 Tbsp chopped fresh basil
- ½ tsp salt
- ½ tsp fresh ground black pepper

DIRECTIONS:

1. Warm oil in a large skillet over medium heat, add sausage and cover. Cook until browned, turning once. After the sausage is brown, add potatoes, onion, salt and pepper. Cover. Stir often.
2. Remove sausage when mostly cooked through. Spread potato mixture across the skillet and cook for about 9 minutes, stirring occasionally.
3. Slice sausage into ½" pieces and return to the pan. Add rosemary, garlic and ½ of the tomatoes. Cook for about 7 minutes; or until tomatoes are cooked. Add basil, remaining tomatoes and stir to combine. Serve and enjoy!

This recipe is AMAZING! If you remember the sitcom, "The Cosby Show", the character Theo talked about how he went to a friend's house, and the mother made Pulpeta (Pull-pay-ta). I ALWAYS wanted to find out what it was. (Because he made it sound SOOO good!) Well, I figured it out! I spoke to a friend who has knowledge in Cuban cuisine, added my own touch and here is the result! I know you're going to like it!

Pulpeta

- 1 cup seasoned bread crumbs
- 2.5 pounds of ground turkey
- 2 beaten eggs
- 1 tsp salt
- 1 tsp pepper
- ½ tsp. basil
- 2 hard boiled eggs
- Another cup seasoned bread crumbs
- 2 more beaten eggs
- ½ cup canola oil
- 1 yellow onion, finely chopped
- ½ green bell pepper, finely chopped
- ½ cup red bell pepper, finely chopped
- 2 cloves garlic, crushed
- 2 large cans tomato sauce
- 1 bay leaf

1) In a large bowl, combine the ground meat (I used ground turkey. But, use whatever ground meat that you like!), ground chicken (again, some people use ground pork).

2) Boil 2 eggs.

3) Add 1 cup of breadcrumbs to the meat, 2 beaten eggs, salt, pepper, basil and knead it together until it's thoroughly combined.

4) Shape this mixture into an oblong loaf.

5) Take the 2 hard-boiled eggs and push them into the loaf, so that they end up right in the center of the loaf, end to end. Shape the meat back into its oblong shape.

6) Refrigerate for at least an hour.

7) Put the rest of the bread crumbs on a flat plate.

8) Put the other 2 beaten eggs on another plate.

9) Carefully roll the loaf in the beaten eggs, then roll in the bread crumbs. Repeat.

10) In a large shallow frying pan, gently brown the loaf on all sides in olive oil. You are basically searing the outside until it creates a nice, crunchy crust.

11) In a pot with a heavy bottom, heat the olive oil and add the garlic, peppers and onions. Cook until soft. Add tomato sauce, white wine, pimientos, peas and bay leaf.

12) Gently place the seared meat into this mixture and reduce heat to low.

13) Cover and simmer over low heat for about 45 minutes to 1 hour. Spoon the sauce over the meat occasionally as it cooks.

14) Remove the meat to a serving platter and allow it to rest.

15) Pour sauce over meat if desired.

Sweet Treats

Bobbie's Pecan Banana Muffins

Ingredients:

2 cups of flour

2 teaspoons of cinnamon

1 ½ teaspoon baking powder

1 teaspoon baking soda

¼ teaspoon salt

4 ripe bananas *mashed*

1 cup of sugar

2 eggs

2 teaspoons of vanilla

½ cup canola oil

Instructions

1. Preheat your oven to 375°F. Line a muffin pan with paper liners.
2. Combine flour, cinnamon, baking soda, baking powder, and salt in a large bowl.
3. In a separate bowl, mix together mashed bananas, sugar, egg, vanilla and canola oil. Add in flour mixture and stir well. (Try not to overmix) Divide batter evenly over 18 muffin cups.
4. Bake for 20-25 minutes or until a toothpick comes out clean. Enjoy!

Bobbie's Yummy Chocolate Brownies

Ingredients:

- 1 cup of butter
- 1 teaspoon canola oil
- 1 cup of brown sugar
- 1 cup of chocolate chips (melted)
- ½ cup of cocoa powder
- 2 teaspoons of vanilla
- 3 large eggs
- 1 cup of Flour
- ½ teaspoon of baking soda
- ½ teaspoon of baking powder
- 1 teaspoon of salt

Directions:

1. Preheat the oven to 375 degrees F. Grease a 9x13-inch pan. ...
2. Combine the melted chocolate, canola oil, butter, sugar, cocoa powder, vanilla, eggs, flour, baking powder, and salt. Mix well.
3. Add the mixture to your 9x13 inch pan.
4. Bake in a preheated oven for 25 minutes or until a toothpick inserted in the center comes out with crumbs, not wet.
5. Cut into equal squares. Enjoy!

Thank you so much for your support! It means the world to us! We hope that these recipes will be a part of your cooking experience for a long time!

www.ingramcontent.com/pod-product-compliance
Lightning Source LLC
Chambersburg PA
CBHW050618110426

42813CB00008B/2601